Livewire
Shakespeare

William Shakesp

RICHARD III

EDITED BY
Philip Page and Marilyn Pettit

ILLUSTRATED BY
Philip Page

Published in association with

The
Basic Skills
Agency

Hodder Murray
A MEMBER OF THE HODDER HEADLINE GROUP

Hodder Headline's policy is to use papers that are natural, renewable and recyclable products and made from wood grown in sustainable forests. The logging and manufacturing processes are expected to conform to the environmental regulations of the country of origin.

Orders: please contact Bookpoint Ltd, 130 Milton Park, Abingdon, Oxon OX14 4SB. Telephone: (44) 01235 827720. Fax: (44) 01235 400454. Lines are open 9.00 – 5.00, Monday to Saturday, with a 24-hour message answering service. Visit our website at www.hoddereducation.co.uk

Text copyright © 2005 Philip Page and Marilyn Pettit
Illustrations copyright © 2005 Philip Page
First published in 2005 by
Hodder Murray, an imprint of Hodder Education,
a member of the Hodder Headline Group
338 Euston Road
London NW1 3BH

Impression number   10 9 8 7 6 5 4 3
Year   2010 2009 2008 2007 2006

Cover photo © Dean and Chapter 1997 photographer: York Glazier's Trust
Typeset by DC Graphic Design Limited, Swanley, Kent
Printed in Great Britain by Martins the Printers, Berwick upon Tweed

A catalogue record for this title is available from the British Library

ISBN-10: 0340 88811 3
ISBN-13: 978 0340 88811 7

Contents

About the play

Richard III is a play about a real historical person. At one time, the play's title was *The Tragedy of Richard III*. A Shakespearian tragedy always has a tragic hero who has a tragic flaw. This means there is something wrong with the central character and this causes his downfall usually a gory death!

As you read the play, decide what Richard's tragic flaw might be. It could be ambition, greed or a love of all things evil! Some people who study history believe that Shakespeare's Richard is different from the real Richard. Others think that he wasn't as evil; and some say he did not murder the princes in the Tower.

In this play, however, Richard plots, arranges murders, lies, manipulates people and eventually pays the price for his evil-doings. He even begins the play by saying he is determined to be a villain! On the way, he is helped by some of his followers, while others hate him and wish he had never been born.

As you read, decide how successful he is as a villain. Does he have any qualities you admire?

Cast of characters

King Edward IV

Queen Elizabeth

Prince Edward Duke of York
Children of the King and Queen.

George, Duke of Clarence

Richard, Duke of Gloucester
King Edward's brothers.

Duchess of York
King Edward's
mother.

Lord Rivers

Lord Grey
Queen Elizabeth's relatives.

Marquis of Dorset

Lady Anne
Widow of King Henry VI's son.

Queen Margaret
Widow of King Henry VI.

Lord Hastings

Duke of Buckingham

**Lord Stanley,
Earl of Derby**

**Sir William
Catesby**

**Sir Richard
Ratcliffe**

Sir James Tyrell

**Sir Robert
Brakenbury**
Lieutenant of the
Tower of London

**The Mayor of
London**

**Two murderers
hired by Richard.**

Earl of Richmond

Duke of Norfolk

Archbishop of York

Richard, Duke of Gloucester, tells us that the fighting between the House of York and the House of Lancaster is over. However, he is not happy that his side's victory has brought peace to the country.

Now is the winter of our discontent made glorious summer by this **son of York**...

And all the clouds that **lour'd** upon our **House** in the deep bosom of the ocean buried.

Now are our brows bound with victorious wreaths, our **bruised arms** hung up for monuments, our stern alarums chang'd to merry meetings, our dreadful marches to delightful **measures**.

Grim-**visag'd** War hath smooth'd his wrinkled front; and now, instead of mounting barbed steeds to fright the souls of fearful adversaries, he capers nimbly in a lady's chamber, to the lascivious pleasing of a lute.

son of York – King Edward IV   **lour'd** – frowned   **House** – House of York   **bruised arms** – battered weapons
measures – dances   **visag'd** – faced

Richard explains why he has chosen to plot against his brothers.

But I, that am not shap'd for **sportive tricks**,   courting
Nor made to court an amorous looking-glass;
I, that am rudely stamp'd, and **want love's majesty**   without the looks
To strut before a wanton ambling nymph:
I, that am curtail'd of this fair proportion,
Cheated of feature by dissembling Nature,
Deform'd, unfinish'd, sent before my time
Into this breathing world scarce half made up—
And that so lamely and unfashionable
That dogs bark at me, as I **halt** by them—   limp
Why, I, in this weak piping time of peace,
Have no delight to pass away the time,
Unless to spy my shadow in the sun,
And **descant on** mine own deformity.   talk about
And therefore, since I cannot prove a lover
To entertain these fair well-spoken days,
I am determined to prove a villain,
And hate the idle pleasures of these days.
Plots have I laid, **inductions** dangerous,   plans
By drunken prophecies, libels, and dreams,
To set my brother Clarence and the King
In deadly hate, the one against the other:
And if King Edward be as true and just
As I am subtle, false and treacherous,
This day should Clarence closely be **mew'd up**   imprisoned
About a prophecy, which says that 'G'
Of Edward's heirs the murderer shall be—
Dive, thoughts, down to my soul: here Clarence comes.

Think about it

What reasons does Richard give for choosing to be a villain?
Do you feel any sympathy for him?

Brother, good day; what means this armed guard?

His Majesty hath appointed this to convey me to **the Tower**.

Upon what cause?

Because my name is George.

He says a wizard told him that by 'G' his **issue** disinherited should be. And for my name begins with G, it follows in his thoughts that I am he.

That fault is none of yours.

'Tis not the King that sends you to the Tower. My Lady Grey, his wife, 'tis she. We are not safe, Clarence, we are not safe!

I think there is no man secure but the Queen's **kindred**.

I will unto the King. Your imprisonment shall not be long: I will deliver you or else lie for you. Have patience.

Simple, plain Clarence, I do love thee so that I will shortly send thy soul to Heaven.

the Tower – the Tower of London
issue – children **kindred** – relatives

But who comes here? The new-deliver'd Hastings?

Good day my gracious lord. What news?

The King is sickly, weak and melancholy, and his physicians fear him mightily.

Where is he? In his bed?

He is.

Go you before, and I will follow you.

He cannot live, I hope, and must not die till George be pack'd up to Heaven. I'll urge his hatred more to Clarence with lies; if I fail not in my deep intent, Clarence hath not another day to live...

...which done, God take King Edward to his mercy and leave the world for me to bustle in.

Then I'll marry **Warwick's youngest daughter**, not for love as for another secret close intent.

But I run before my horse to market: Clarence still breathes, Edward still lives and reigns; when they are gone, then must I count my gains.

Warwick's youngest daughter – Lady Anne

4

Act 1 Scene 2

Lady Anne follows the coffin of King Henry VI. She curses Richard.

Poor key-cold Figure of a holy king, pale ashes of the House of Lancaster. Hear the lamentations of poor Anne, wife to thy slaughter'd son, stabbed by the selfsame hand that made these wounds.

Cursed be the hand that made these holes! Cursed the heart that had the heart to do it!

If ever he have wife, let her be made more miserable by the death of him than I am made by my young lord and thee!

Set down the **corse**, or I'll make a corse of him that disobeys!

corse – corpse

5

| Act 1 Scene 2 | Anne accuses Richard of killing her husband. He pretends he did it because he loves her. |

go away

Anne: Avaunt, thou dreadful minister of hell!
Thou had'st but power over his mortal body:
His soul thou canst not have; therefore begone.
Thou hast made the happy earth thy hell.

Richard: I did not kill your husband.

Anne: Why then he is alive.

Richard: Nay he is dead, and slain by Edward's hand.

Anne: Thou liest. Didst thou not kill this King?

Richard: I grant ye, yea.

Anne: He is in Heaven, and thou unfit for any place but
    hell.

Richard: One place else. Your bed-chamber.
Is not the causer of the deaths of Henry and Edward
As blameful as the executioner?

Anne: Thou wast the cause, and most accurs'd effect.

Richard: Your beauty was the cause of that effect.

Anne: If I thought that, I tell thee, homicide,
These nails should **rend** that beauty from my cheeks.   rip
I would I were reveng'd on thee.

Richard: It is a quarrel most unnatural
    To be reveng'd on him that loveth thee.

6

Anne: To be reveng'd on him that kill'd my husband.
   His better doth not breathe upon the earth.

Richard: He lives that loves thee better than he could.

Anne: Where is he?

Richard: Here.   [*She spits at him*]

Anne: Out of my sight! Thou dost infect mine eye.

Richard: Lady, if thy revengeful heart cannot forgive,
Here I lend thee this sharp-pointed sword,
Which if thou please to hide in this true breast.
Nay, do not pause, for I did kill King Henry—
But 'twas thy beauty that provoked me.
Take up the sword again or take up me.

Anne: I will not be thy executioner.

Richard: Shall I live in hope? **Vouchsafe** to wear this ring.   agree

Anne: To take is not to give.

Richard: Look how my ring encompasseth thy finger:
Even so thy breast encloseth my poor heart.
After I have solemnly **interr'd** this noble King,   buried
I will see you.

Anne: Much it joys me to see you are become so penitent.
                  [*Exit*]

Richard: Was ever woman in this humour woo'd?
   Was ever woman in this humour won? I'll have her,
   but I will not keep her long.

Think about it

What do you think is Richard's real motive when he declares his love for her?

Act 1
Scene 3

The Queen is worried about her future and quarrels with Richard.

Madam, no doubt his Majesty will soon recover his health.

If he were dead, what would betide on me?

The heavens have bless'd you with a son to be your comforter when he is gone.

He is young, and put unto the trust of Richard Gloucester, a man that loves me not, nor none of you.

Saw you the King today?

Ay, he desires to make **atonement** between the Duke of Gloucester and your brothers.

That will never be.

Who is it that complains unto the King that I love them not? Because I cannot flatter, and look fair, I must be held an enemy.

To who speaks your Grace?

To thee. His royal Grace cannot be quiet scarce a breathing while but you must trouble him with lewd complaints.

atonement – peace

8

You mistake the matter: the King, not provok'd by any suitor, makes him to send, that he may learn the ground of your ill will and remove it.

You envy my advancement, and my friends'.

Our brother is imprison'd by your means, myself disgrac'd.

I never did incense his Majesty against the Duke of Clarence.

My lord of Gloucester, I have too long borne your bitter scoffs; I will acquaint his Majesty of those gross taunts that oft I have endur'd.

What, threat you me with telling of the King? Tell him: look what I have said I will **avouch't** in presence of the King. 'Tis time to speak.

avouch't – stand by what I've said

9

<table>
<tr><td>Act 1
Scene 3</td><td>Richard justifies what he has done. Margaret eavesdrops and then tells him what she thinks of him!</td></tr>
</table>

Richard: Ere you were queen, or your husband king,
I was a pack-horse in his great affairs;
A weeder-out of his proud adversaries;
A liberal rewarder of his friends:
To royalize his blood, I spent mine own.

Margaret: [*Aside*] Ay, and much better blood than his, or
thine.

Richard: In all which time, you and your husband Grey
Were **factious** for the House of Lancaster: supporters
And Rivers, so were you. Was not your husband
In Margaret's battle at Saint Albans slain?
Let me put in your minds, if you forget,
What you have been ere this, and what you are;
Withal, what I have been, and what I am.

Margaret: [*Aside*] A murd'rous villain, and so still thou art.

Richard: Poor Clarence did forsake his father and
forswore himself
To fight on Edward's party for the crown:
And for his meed, he is mew'd up.
I would to God my heart were flint, like Edward's,
Or Edward's soft and pitiful, like mine.
I am too childish-foolish for this world.

Margaret: [*Aside*] Hie thee to hell for shame, and leave
this world,
Thou **cacodemon**: there thy kingdom is.   evil spirit

Rivers: My lord of Gloucester, in those busy days
Which here you urge to prove us enemies,
We follow'd then our lord, our sovereign king:
So should we you, if you should be our king.

Richard: If I should be? I had rather be a pedlar!
Far be it from my heart, the thought thereof.

Margaret: I can no longer hold me patient!
Which of you trembles not, that looks on me?
Villain! do not turn away.

Richard: Foul, wrinkled witch, what mak'st thou in my
  sight?

Margaret: Repetition of what thou hast marr'd:
That will I make, before I let thee go.

Richard: Wert thou not banished on pain of death?

Margaret: I was, but I do find more pain in banishment
Than death can yield me here by my abode.
A husband and a son thou ow'st to me;
And thou a kingdom.
This sorrow that I have by right is yours;
And all the pleasures you usurp are mine.

Think about it

How dramatic would this scene be on stage
when Margaret speaks out?

Rivers and Dorset, you were standers-by, and so wast thou, Lord Hastings, when **my son** was stabb'd with bloody daggers.

Have done, thou hateful wither'd hag.

And leave out thee? Dog, thou shalt hear me.

No sleep close up that deadly eye of thine, unless it be while some tormenting dream affrights thee with a hell of ugly devils. Thou elvish-mark'd, abortive, rooting hog.

Poor painted queen, the day will come that thou shalt wish for me to help thee curse this poisonous bunch-back'd toad.

End thy frantic curse.

She is lunatic.

Take heed of yonder dog! When he **fawns**, he bites; and when he bites his venom tooth will rankle to the death. Beware of him; sin, death, and hell have set their marks on him.

my son – Lady Anne's husband
fawns – shows affection

My hair doth stand on end to hear her curses.

I muse why she's at liberty.

I cannot blame her: she hath had too much wrong; and I repent my part that I have done to her. As for Clarence, he is well repaid.

Madam, his Majesty doth call for you, and you my gracious lords.

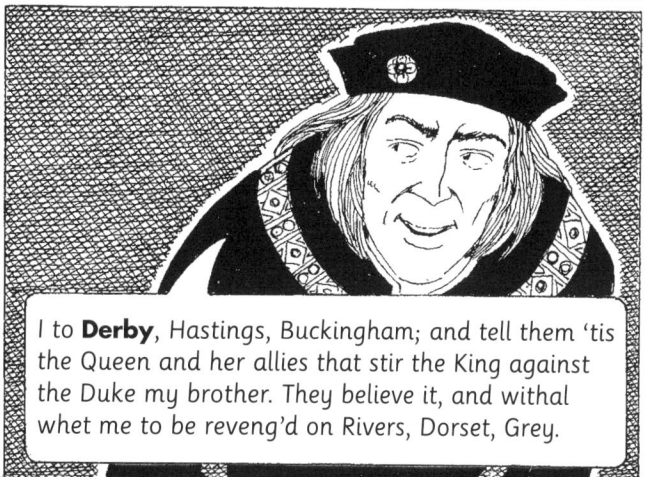

I to **Derby**, Hastings, Buckingham; and tell them 'tis the Queen and her allies that stir the King against the Duke my brother. They believe it, and withal whet me to be reveng'd on Rivers, Dorset, Grey.

Here come my executioners. Are you going to dispatch this thing?

We are, my lord, come to have the warrant.

I have it here. Be sudden in the execution: do not hear him plead; for Clarence is well-spoken and may move your hearts to pity.

We will not stand to **prate**. We go to use our hands, and not our tongues.

Derby – Lord Stanley
prate – chatter

13

The murderers Richard has hired kill Clarence in the Tower.

Why looks your Grace so heavily today?

I have passed a miserable night, so full of fearful dreams.

Methoughts I had broken from the Tower, and embark'd to cross to Burgundy; and in my company my brother Gloucester. Gloucester stumbled, and in falling struck me overboard, into the tumbling **billows of the main**.

O Lord! Methought what pain it was to drown: what dreadful noise of waters in my ears. Methoughts I saw a thousand fearful wrecks; ten thousand men that fishes gnaw'd upon, all scatter'd in the bottom of the sea.

My soul is heavy, and I would sleep.

What woulds't thou?

Let him see our commission.

I am in this commanded to deliver the Duke of Clarence to your hands.

There lies the Duke asleep. I'll to the King, and signify to him that thus I have resigned to you my charge.

billows of the main – waves of the sea

14

Art thou afraid?

Not to kill him, but to be damned for killing him.

Remember our reward.

I had forgot the reward.

Where's thy conscience now?

In the Duke of Gloucester's purse.

When he opens his purse to give us our reward, thy conscience flies out.

He wakes.

Wherefore do you come? To murder me?

Ay.

What is my offence? Where is the evidence that doth accuse me?

What we will do, we do upon command.

And he that hath commanded is our king.

The great King of kings hath commanded thou shalt do no murder.

Thou dids't **receive the sacrament** to fight in quarrel of the House of Lancaster.

And dids't break that vow, and unrip'st the bowels of thy sovereign's son.

If you are hir'd, I will send you to my brother Gloucester, who shall reward you better for my life than Edward will for tidings of my death.

For whose sake did I that ill deed? For Edward, my brother, for his sake.

Your brother Gloucester hates you.

O, no, he loves me.

'Tis he that sends us to destroy you here.

Take that!

If all this will not do, I'll drown you in the **malmsey-butt** within.

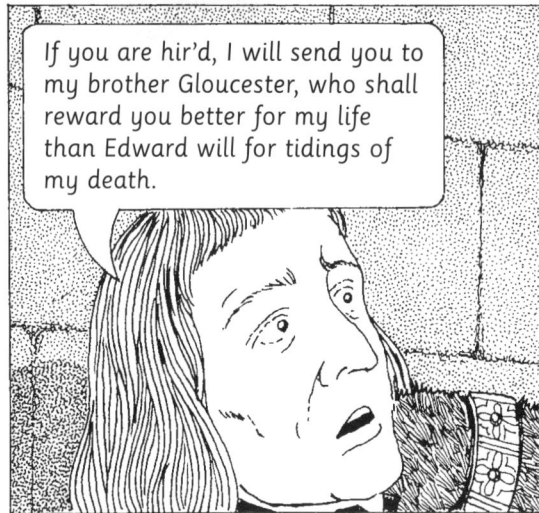

receive the sacrament – solemnly promise
malmsey-butt – wine barrel

16

King Edward is ill and tries to make peace between the nobles – but Richard has other plans.

Now have I done a good day's work: you peers, swear your love. You have been factious, one against the other.

Wife, love Lord Hastings, let him kiss your hand.

Buckingham, seal thou this league with thy embracements to my wife's allies.

There wanteth now our brother Gloucester here to make the blessed period of this peace.

Good morrow to my sovereign King and Queen.

Gloucester, we have made peace of enmity, fair love of hate, between these peers.

A blessed labour, my most sovereign lord. If any here by false intelligence or wrong surmise hold me a foe, I desire to reconcile me to his friendly peace.

I do beseech your Highness to take our brother Clarence to your grace.

Madam, have I offered love for this? Who knows not that the gentle Duke is dead? You do him injury to scorn his corse!

Clarence dead? The order was revers'd.

But he, poor man, by your first order died.

Who sued to me for him? None of you would once beg for his life. Poor Clarence!

Mark'd you not how that the guilty kindred of the Queen look'd pale when they did hear of Clarence's death? O, they did urge it still unto the King: God will revenge it.

Clarence's children ask about their father's death. News comes of King Edward's death, which leads to further plots!

dissemble – lie

Panel 1: Edward, my lord, thy son, our King, is dead.

Panel 2: Madam, bethink you, like a careful mother, of the young prince your son. Send straight for him; let him be crown'd.

Panel 3: Sister, have comfort. None can help our harms by wailing them.

Panel 4: My mother: I did not see your Grace. I crave your blessing.

Panel 5: Cheer each other. Though we have spent our harvest of this king, we are to reap the harvest of his son. With **some little train**, forthwith from Ludlow the young Prince be fet to London, to be crown'd our King.

Why with some little train?

Panel 6: Lest by a multitude the new-heal'd wound of malice should break out.

I hope the King made peace with all of us, the **compact** is firm and true in me.

some little train – a small group of people
compact – agreement

20

And so in me: yet since it is but green, **it should be put to no apparent likelihood of breach**. It is meet so few should fetch the Prince.

Whoever journeys to the Prince, let not us two stay at home: by the way I'll sort occasion as index to the story we late talk'd of, to part the Queen's proud kindred from the Prince.

Towards Ludlow then, for we'll not stay behind.

Act 2 Scene 3 | Three citizens of London talk about the news of King Edward's death. They are worried about the future.

Doth the news hold of good King Edward's death?

Ay, sir, it is true.

Woe to that land that's govern'd by a child.

His son shall reign.

Truly, the hearts of men are full of fear: you cannot reason almost with a man that looks not heavily and full of dread.

it should...of breach – it should not be put at risk

The Queen learns of her relatives' arrest and fears for her own safety.

Tomorrow, or next day, they will be here.

I long with all my heart to see the Prince; I hope he is much grown since last I saw him.

Here comes a messenger.

What news?

Lord Rivers and Lord Grey are sent to Pomfret, and with them Sir Thomas Vaughan, prisoners.

Who hath committed them?

The mighty Dukes, Gloucester and Buckingham.

For what offence?

Why or for what is all unknown to me, my gracious lord.

I see the ruin of my House: the tiger now hath seiz'd the gentle **hind**. We will to **sanctuary**.

I will go with you.

I'll conduct you to the sanctuary.

hind – a female deer
sanctuary – a place of safety in a church

Prince Edward is welcomed to London by his uncle, Richard, who suggests that he and his brother stay in the Tower until the coronation.

Welcome, sweet Prince, to London.

Welcome, dear cousin.

I want more uncles here to welcome me.

Sweet Prince, the **untainted** virtue of your years hath not yet div'd into the world's deceit. Those uncles which you want were dangerous; Your Grace attended to their sugar'd words, but look'd not on the poison of their hearts.

I thought my mother and my brother York would have met us on the way. What a slug is Hastings, that he comes not to tell us whether they will come or no.

Here comes the sweating lord.

untainted – unspoilt

The Queen your mother and your brother York have taken sanctuary. The tender prince would have come to meet your Grace, but by his mother was perforce withheld.

Lord Cardinal, will your Grace persuade the Queen to send the Duke of York unto his princely brother presently?

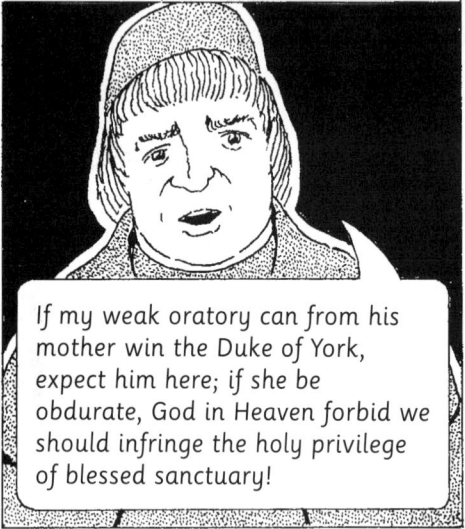

If my weak oratory can from his mother win the Duke of York, expect him here; if she be obdurate, God in Heaven forbid we should infringe the holy privilege of blessed sanctuary!

The Prince hath neither claim'd it nor deserv'd it: and therefore cannot have it; you break no privilege.

My lord, you shall o'er-rule my mind for once. Come, Lord Hastings, will you go with me?

Uncle Gloucester, if our brother come, where shall we **sojourn** till our coronation?

Some day or two at the Tower, then where you please.

I do not like the Tower.

sojourn – stay

24

Here comes the Duke of York.

Richard of York: how fares our loving brother?

Well, my dread lord – so must I call you now.

How fares our cousin, noble lord of York?

I thank you, gentle uncle.

My lord, myself and my good cousin Buckingham will to your mother, to entreat of her to meet you at the Tower and welcome you.

What, will you go unto the Tower, my lord?

My **Lord Protector** needs will have it so.

I shall not sleep in quiet at the Tower.

Why, what should you fear?

My uncle Clarence's angry ghost: my grandam told me he was murder'd there.

I fear no uncles dead.

Nor none that live, hope?

Lord Protector – Richard

25

Catesby. Is it not an easy matter to make Lord Hastings of our mind for the instalment of this noble Duke in the seat royal of this famous isle?

He so loves the Prince that he will not be won to aught against him.

What of Stanley? Will not he?

Sound thou Lord Hastings how he doth stand affected to our purpose, summon him tomorrow to the Tower to sit about the coronation. If thou dost find him **tractable** to us, encourage him, and tell him all our reasons. If he be unwilling, break off the talk, and give us notice.

He will do all in all as Hastings doth.

Shall we hear from you, Catesby, ere we sleep?

You shall, my lord.

What shall we do if Lord Hastings will not yield to our **complots**?

Chop off his head.

When I am king, claim thou of me the earldom of Hereford.

I'll claim that promise at your Grace's hand.

tractable – agreeable/sympathetic
complots – plans

**Act 3
Scene 2**

Catesby sounds out Lord Hastings, who does not realise the danger he is in.

[*Enter a* Messenger *to the Door of Lord Hastings*]

Hastings: Who knocks?

Messenger: One from the Lord Stanley. This night he dreamt the boar had **razed off his helm**; he says there are two Councils kept, and that may be determin'd at the one which may make you and him to rue at th'other.

chopped off his helmet

Hastings: Bid him not fear: his honour and myself are at the one, and at the other is my good friend Catesby, nothing can proceed that toucheth us whereof I shall not have intelligence. Go, bid thy master rise and we will both together to the Tower, where he shall see the boar will use us kindly.

[*The* Messenger *leaves*]

[*Enter* Catesby]

Hastings: Good morrow, Catesby; what news?

Catesby: It is a reeling world, my lord, and I believe will never stand upright till Richard wear the garland of the realm.

Hastings: Dost thou mean the crown?

Catesby: Ay.

Hastings: I'll have this crown of mine cut from my shoulders before I'll see the crown so foul misplac'd. But canst thou guess that he doth aim at it?

Catesby: Ay, and hopes to find you forward upon his party for the gain thereof. He sends you good news that this very day your enemies, the kindred of the Queen, must die at Pomfret.

Hastings: I am no mourner for that news: but that I'll give my voice on Richard's side, I will not do it.

Catesby: God keep your lordship in that gracious mind.

Hastings: But I shall laugh at this a twelve-month hence, That they which brought me in my master's hate, I live to look upon their tragedy.

Catesby: 'Tis a vile thing to die, my gracious lord, when men are unprepar'd and look not for't.

Hastings: O, monstrous, monstrous! And so falls it out with Rivers, Vaughan, Grey: and so 'twill do with some men else that think themselves as safe as thou and I, who as thou know'st are dear to princely Richard and to Buckingham.

Catesby: The Princes both make high account of you— [*Aside*] For they account his head upon the **Bridge**.   London Bridge

Hastings: I know they do, and I have well deserv'd it.

Think about it

Look at Hastings' last line. What does he think he has deserved? How is this different from Catesby's view?

Tower – the Tower of London

Act 3 Scene 3

Ratcliffe supervises the execution of the Queen's supporters.

Bring forth the prisoners.

Now Margaret's curse is fall'n upon our heads for standing by when Richard stabb'd her son.

Then curs'd she Richard, then curs'd she Buckingham, then curs'd she Hastings.

Make haste: the hour of death **is expiate**.

Farewell, until we meet again in Heaven.

is expiate – is here

30

Hastings discovers that Richard will not let anybody oppose him or his plans.

Hastings: We are met to determine the coronation.
When is the royal day?

Buckingham: Who knows the Lord Protector's mind
herein?
Who is most inward with the noble Duke?
Lord Hastings, you and he are near in love.

Hastings: I thank his Grace, I know he loves me well;
But for his purpose in the coronation
I have not sounded him, nor he deliver'd
His gracious pleasure any way therein.
But you, my honourable lords, may name the time,
And in the Duke's behalf I'll give my voice,
Which I presume he'll take in gentle part.
[*Enter* Richard]

Buckingham: Had you not come upon your cue, my lord,
Lord Hastings had pronounc'd your part—
I mean your voice for crowning of the King.

Richard: His lordship knows me well, and loves me well.
Buckingham, a word with you.
Catesby hath sounded Hastings in our business,
And finds the **testy** gentleman so hot   irritable
That he will lose his head ere give consent
His master's child shall lose the throne.
[*Exit* Richard *and* Buckingham]

Hastings: His Grace looks cheerfully and smooth today.
I think there's never a man in Christendom
Can lesser hide his love or hate than he,
For by his face straight shall you know his heart.

Stanley: What of his heart perceive you in his face today?

Hastings: That with no man here he is offended.
                    [*Enter* Richard *and* Buckingham]

Richard: I pray you all, tell me what they deserve
That do conspire my death with devilish plots
Of damned witchcraft, and that have prevail'd
Upon my body with their hellish charms?

Hastings: Whatso'er they be, my lord, they have deserv'd
    death.

Richard: Then be your eyes the witness of their evil.
See how I am bewitch'd! Behold, mine arm
Is like a blasted sapling wither'd up!
And this Edward's wife, that monstrous witch,
Consorted with that harlot, strumpet **Shore**
That by their witchcraft thus have mark'd me.

Jane Shore was King Edward IV's mistress.

Hastings: If they have done this deed, my noble Lord—

Richard: If? Thou protector of this damned strumpet,
Talk'st thou to me of ifs! Thou art a traitor:
Off with his head! Now by Saint Paul I swear
I will not dine until I see the same.
Lovell and Ratcliffe, look that it be done;
The rest that love me, rise and follow me.
                    [*Exit all but* Lovell, Ratcliffe *and* Hastings]

Hastings: O bloody Richard! Miserable England.
Come, lead me to the block: bear him my head.
They smile at me who shortly shall be dead.

Think about it

What do you think about Hastings' last three lines?

Go after the Mayor. Infer the bastardy of Edward's children. Urge his bestial appetite in change of lust, which stretch'd unto their servants, daughters, wives, even where his raging eye or savage heart without control lusted to make a prey.

Tell them, when that my mother went with child of that insatiate Edward, noble York my princely father, then had wars in France, and by true computation of the time found that the issue was not his-begot, which well appeared in his **lineaments**, being nothing like the noble Duke, my father.

Yet touch this sparingly, as 'twere far off, because, my lord you know my mother lives.

I'll play the orator.

Now will I go to draw the brats of Clarence out of sight, and to give notice that no person have, at any time, recourse unto the Princes.

Act 3 Scene 6

A clerk comments on the speed of Lord Hastings' fall from power and his execution. He worries about the future.

Here is the indictment of good Lord Hastings. Eleven hours I have spent to write it, for yesternight by Catesby was it sent to me...

...and yet within these five hours Hastings liv'd, **untainted**, **unexamin'd**, free, at liberty. Bad is the world, and all will come to naught when such ill-dealing must be seen in thought.

lineaments – features
untainted – innocent
unexamin'd – not tried

Act 3 Scene 7

Buckingham tries to get support from the people of London for Richard to be made King. It is not an easy task!

What say the citizens?

Not a word.

Touch'd you the bastardy of Edward's children?

I did, and his own bastardy.

I did infer your lineaments, laid open all your victories in Scotland, your discipline in war, wisdom in peace, your bounty, virtue, fair humility. I bid them that did love their country's good cry, 'God save Richard, England's royal King!'

And did they so?

They spake not a word.

I asked the Mayor what meant this silence. His answer was the people were not us'd to be spoke to but by the Recorder. He was urg'd to tell my tale again.

When he had done, some followers of mine hurl'd up their caps, and some ten voices cried 'God save King Richard!'

Recorder – city magistrate

35

The Mayor is here at hand. Intend some fear; get a prayer-book in your hand, stand between two churchmen.

Be not easily won to our requests: play the maid's part: still answer nay, and take it.

Welcome, my lord. I think the Duke will not be spoke withal.

Catesby, what says your lord to my request?

He is within, with two reverend fathers, divinely bent to meditation.

Return, good Catesby, to the gracious Duke; tell him myself, the Mayor and aldermen, are come to have some conference with his Grace.

My lord, this prince is not an Edward lolling on a lewd love-bed, but on his knees at meditation, praying. Happy were England, would this virtuous Prince take on the sovereignty thereof. But I fear we shall not win him to it.

God defend his Grace should say us nay!

Be not easily...and take it. – Pretend you don't want to be King.

36

Here Catesby comes again. What says his Grace?

He fears, my lord, you mean no good to him.

We come to him in perfect love: return and tell his Grace.

What is your Grace's pleasure?

You **resign** the throne, the lineal glory of your royal House, to the corruption of a blemish'd stock. We heartily solicit your gracious self to take on you the kingly government of this your land.

Your love deserves my thanks, but much is my poverty of spirit, so mighty and so many my defects, that I would rather hide me from my greatness.

The royal tree hath left us royal fruit, on him I lay that you would lay on me.

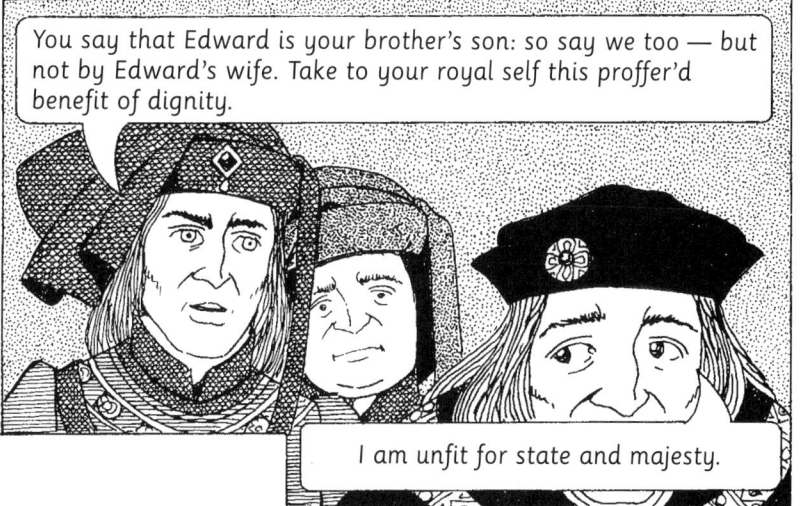

You say that Edward is your brother's son: so say we too — but not by Edward's wife. Take to your royal self this proffer'd benefit of dignity.

I am unfit for state and majesty.

resign – abandon

Know, whe'er you accept our suit or no, your brother's son shall never reign our king, but we will plant some other in the throne to the disgrace and downfall of your House. I'll entreat no more.

Call them again. I am not made of stones.

Cousin of Buckingham, and **sage** grave men, I must have patience to endure the load. God doth know how far I am from the desire of this.

God bless your Grace.

Long live Richard, England's worthy King!

Tomorrow may it please you to be crown'd?

When you please, for you will have it so.

Tomorrow then.

Come, let us to our holy work again.

sage – wise

38

Richard will not let anybody see the Princes and he sends for Anne to come to the coronation.

Master Lieutenant, how doth the Prince and my young son of York?

Well, dear madam. I may not suffer you to visit them: the King hath strictly charg'd the contrary.

The King! Who's that?

I mean the Lord Protector.

The Lord protect him from that kingly title! I am their mother; who shall bar me from them?

I am their father's mother: I will see them.

No, madam, I may not. I am bound by oath.

Madam, you must straight to Westminster, there to be crowned Richard's royal queen.

Despiteful tidings! I with all unwillingness will go.

Go, poor soul, I envy not thy glory.

When he that is my husband now came to me as I follow'd Henry's corse, this was my wish: when thou wed'st, let sorrow haunt thy bed; and be thy wife – if any be so mad – more miserable by the life of thee than thou hast made me by my dear lord's death.

I prov'd the subject of mine own curse.

He hates me, and will, no doubt, shortly be rid of me.

Go thou to Richard, and good angels tend thee.

Look back with me unto the Tower. Pity, you ancient stones, those tender babes **immur'd** within your walls – use my babies well.

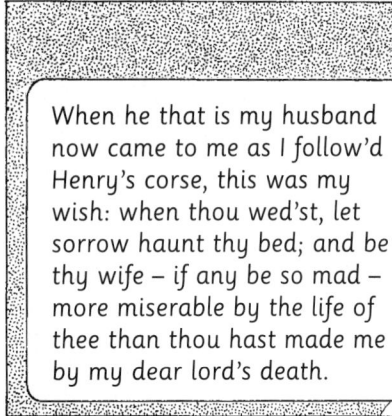

immur'd – imprisoned

King Richard is anxious about his future security and arranges to have the Princes killed. Buckingham realises that he is no longer safe.

Cousin of Buckingham. Thus high, by thy advice and thy assistance is King Richard seated.

But shall we wear these glories for a day, or shall they last, and we rejoice in them?

For ever let them last!

I would be King.

Why, so you are.

'Tis so – but **Edward** lives.

True, noble Prince.

I wish the bastards dead.

Give me some breath, dear lord, before I positively speak in this.

High-reaching Buckingham grows **circumspect**.

Boy! Know'st thou any whom corrupting gold will tempt unto a close exploit of death?

I know a discontented gentleman. Gold will tempt him to anything. His name is Tyrrel.

Edward – the Prince of Wales
circumspect – wary/cautious

The **deep-revolving** Buckingham no more shall be the neighbour to my counsels.

Catesby. Rumour it abroad that Anne my wife is grievous sick. Enquire me out some mean poor gentleman, whom I will marry straight to Clarence's daughter – the boy is foolish, and I fear him not. It stands me much upon to stop all hopes whose growth may damage me.

I must be married to my brother's daughter, or else my kingdom stands on brittle glass. Murder her brothers, and then marry her.

I am in so far in blood that sin will pluck on sin; tear-falling pity dwells not in this eye.

Tyrrel? Dar'st thou kill a friend of mine?

I had rather kill two enemies.

Two deep enemies are they that I would have thee deal upon.

I mean those bastards in the Tower.

I'll rid you from the fear of them. I will dispatch it straight.

deep-revolving – over-thoughtful

42

My lord, I have consider'd in my mind the late request that you did sound me in.

Let that rest.

Dorset is fled to Richmond. Stanley, he is your wife's son. Look into it.

My lord, I claim the gift, my due by promise, for which your honour and your faith is pawn'd: th'earldom of Hereford and the **moveables** which you have promised I shall possess.

Stanley, look to your wife; if she convey letters to Richmond, you shall answer it.

What says your Highness to my just demand?

I am not in the giving vein today.

And is it thus? Repays he my deep service with such contempt? Made I him King for this?

Let me think on Hastings, and be gone while my fearful head is on.

moveables – goods/possessions

43

**Act 4
Scene 3**

Richard continues to plot but receives alarming news about Buckingham and Richmond.

The tyrannous and bloody act is done; the gentle babes smothered.

But did'st thou see them dead?

I did, my lord.

And buried?

The chaplain of the Tower hath buried them, but where, I do not know.

Tyrrel, think how I may do thee good, farewell till then.

The son of Clarence have I **pent up** close; his daughter meanly have I match'd in marriage; the sons of Edward sleep in Abraham's bosom, and Anne my wife hath bid this world good night.

Now, for I know the **Breton** Richmond aims at young Elizabeth, my brother's daughter, and by that **knot** looks proudly on the crown to her go I, a jolly thriving wooer.

My lord! Buckingham is in the field, and still his power increaseth.

Go **muster** men. My counsel is my shield. We must be brief, when traitors brave the field.

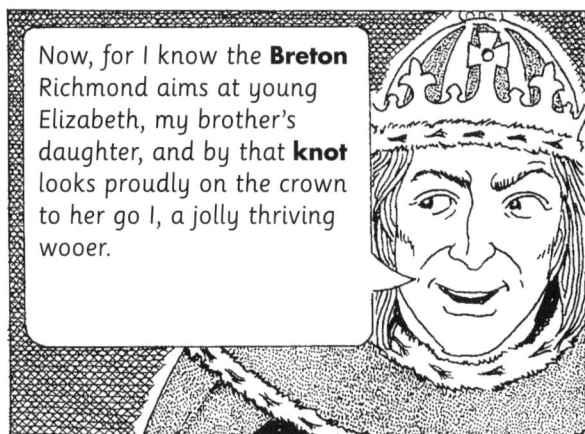

pent up – locked up
Breton – somebody from Brittany, France
knot – marriage
muster – gather

44

Elizabeth and Richard's mother confront him, but Richard has another plan to secure his position as King.

Richard: Who intercepts me in my expedition?

Duchess: She that might have intercepted thee—
By strangling thee in her accursed womb—
From all the slaughters, wretch, that thou hast done.

Queen Elizabeth: Hid'st thou that forehead with a
golden crown
Where should be branded, if that right were right,
The slaughter of the Prince that ow'd that crown,
And the dire death of my poor sons and brothers?
Tell me, thou villain-slave, where are my children?

Duchess: Toad, thou toad, where is thy brother Clarence,
And little Ned Plantagenet his son?

Queen Elizabeth: Where is the gentle Rivers, Vaughan
and Grey?

Duchess: Where is kind Hastings?

Richard: Let not the heavens hear these tell-tale women.

Duchess: Thou cam'st on earth to make the earth my
hell.
A grievous burden was thy birth to me;
Tetchy and wayward was thy infancy;   nervous/short-tempered
Thy school-days frightful, desp'rate, wild, and furious;
Thy prime of manhood daring, bold, and venturous;
Thy age confirm'd, proud, subtle, sly, and bloody:
More mild, but yet more harmful, kind in hatred.
What comfortable hour canst thou name
That ever grac'd me with thy company?

Richard: If I be so disgracious in your eye,
Let me march on and not offend you, madam.

Duchess: Hear me a word, for I shall never speak to thee
    again.
Take with thee my most grievous curse.
Bloody thou art; bloody will be thy end.
Shame serves thy life and doth thy death attend.
                    [*The* Duchess *leaves*]

Richard: Madam, I must talk a word with you.

Queen Elizabeth: I have no more sons of the royal blood
    for thee to slaughter.

Richard: You have a daughter call'd Elizabeth.

Queen Elizabeth: And must she die for this?

Richard: I love thy daughter and do intend to make her
    Queen of England.

Queen Elizabeth: How canst thou woo her?

Richard: That would I learn of you.

Queen Elizabeth: Send to her, by the man that slew her
    brothers,
A pair of bleeding hearts.
Tell her thou mad'st away her uncle Clarence,
Her uncle Rivers – ay, and for her sake
Mad'st quick conveyance with her good aunt Anne.

Richard: You mock me, madam; this is not the way to
    win your daughter!

Queen Elizabeth: There is no other way—
    Unless thou couldst put on some other shape.

Richard: Say that I did all this for love of her?
If I did take the kingdom from your sons,
To make amends I'll give it to your daughter.

Queen Elizabeth: What were I best to say? Her father's
  brother
Would be her lord? Or shall I say her uncle?
Or he that slew her brothers and her uncle?
Under what title shall I woo for thee?

Richard: Infer fair England's peace by this alliance.
Say she shall be a high and mighty queen.
Say I will love her everlastingly.
Plead what I will be, not what I have been;
Not my deserts, but what I will deserve.

Queen Elizabeth: I go. Write to me very shortly, and you
  shall understand from me her mind.

Richard: Bear her my true love's kiss; and so farewell.
                              [Elizabeth *leaves*]
Relenting fool, and shallow, changing woman.

Think about it

Do you agree with Richard's opinion of
Queen Elizabeth after she leaves the stage?

Panel 1:
What news?

Most mighty sovereign, on the western coast rideth a **puissant** navy.

Panel 2:
'Tis thought Richmond is their admiral, expecting the aid of Buckingham to welcome them ashore.

Panel 3:
Post to the Duke of Norfolk. Bid him **levy** the greatest strength and power he can make and meet me at Salisbury.

Panel 4:
Stanley, what news with you?

Richmond is on the seas. He makes for England here to claim the crown.

Panel 5:
Is the King dead? Where is thy power then to beat him back?

My friends are in the north.

Panel 6:
What do they in the north? Ay, ay, thou wouldst join with Richmond. I'll not trust thee.

Panel 7:
I never was, nor ever will be, false.

Panel 8:
Go then, and muster men – but leave behind your son. Look your heart be firm, or else his head's assurance is but frail.

Panel 9:
My liege, every hour more competitors flock to the rebels, and their power grows strong.

Nothing but songs of death?

puissant – powerful
levy – gather

48

Majesty, Buckingham's army is dispers'd and scatter'd, and he wander'd away, no man knows whither.

Hath any well-advis'd friend proclaim'd reward to him that brings the traitor in?

Such proclamation has been made, my lord.

My liege, the Duke of Buckingham is taken. That is the best news. That Richmond is with a mighty power landed at **Milford** is colder tidings.

Away towards Salisbury!

Act 4 Scene 5   Stanley sends a message to Richmond explaining why he cannot openly take his side yet.

Tell Richmond this from me: that in the sty of the most deadly boar my son George Stanley is **frank'd up in hold**. If I revolt, off goes young George's head: the fear of that holds off my present aid. Say that the Queen hath heartily consented he should **espouse** Elizabeth her daughter. Where is Richmond now?

At Pembroke, or at Ha'rfordwest in Wales. With a valiant crew towards London do they bend their power.

Hie thee to thy lord. My letter will resolve him of my mind.

Milford – Milford Haven
frank'd up in hold – held prisoner
espouse – marry

Buckingham is executed.

Will not King Richard let me speak with him?

Thus Margaret's curse falls heavy on my neck.

No, my good lord.

Come, lead me, officers, to the block of shame; wrong hath but wrong, and blame the due of blame.

Richmond and his army draw closer to Richard.

Fellows in arms, and my most loving friends, bruis'd underneath the yoke of tyranny: thus far have we march'd on without impediment.

The wretched, bloody and usurping boar is now even in the centre of this isle near to the town of Leicester.

From Tamworth thither is but one day's march: in God's name, cheerly on to reap the harvest of perpetual peace by this one bloody trial of sharp war.

Richard prepares for battle, but there are unpleasant surprises in store for him and his supporters before the fighting begins!

Here pitch our tent, here in Bosworth field. Here will I lie tonight.

Who hath descried the number of the traitors?

Six or seven thousand is their utmost power.

Our **battalia** trebles that account! Come, noble gentlemen, make no delay: for, lords, tomorrow is a busy day!

Catesby! Send to Stanley's regiment. Bid him bring his power before sun-rising, lest his son George fall into the blind cave of eternal night.

Ratcliffe! Give me a bowl of wine. I have not that alacrity of spirit nor cheer of mind that I was wont to have.

Bid my guard watch. About the mid of night come and help to arm me.

battalia – army

The ghosts of Richard's victims come
back to haunt him.

Ghost of Prince Edward, son of King Henry VI: Let
   me sit heavy on thy soul tomorrow.
Think how thou stab'st me at Tewkesbury;
Despair, therefore and die.

[*Exit*]

Ghost of Henry VI: When I was mortal, my anointed body
By thee was punched full of deadly holes.
Think on the Tower and me: despair and die;
Harry the Sixth bids thee despair and die.

[*Exit*]

Ghost of Clarence: Let me sit heavy in thy soul
   tomorrow—
I, that was wash'd to death with fulsome wine,
Poor Clarence, by thy guile betray'd to death—
Tomorrow in the battle think on me,
And fall thy edgeless sword; despair and die.

[*Exit*]

Ghost of Rivers: Let me sit heavy in your soul tomorrow,
Rivers that died at Pomfret: despair and die.

Ghost of Grey: Think upon Grey, and let thy soul despair.

Ghost of Vaughan: Think upon Vaughan, and with
   guilty fear
Let fall thy lance; despair and die.

[*Exeunt*]

Ghost of Hastings: Bloody and guilty, guiltily awake,
And in bloody battle end thy days.
Think on Hastings; despair and die.

[*Exit*]

Ghosts of the two young Princes: Dream on thy
      cousins, smother'd in the Tower:
Let us be lead within thy bosom, Richard,
And weigh thee down to ruin, shame, and death;
Thy nephews' souls bid thee despair and die.

                                                          [*Exeunt*]

Ghost of Anne: Richard, thy wife, that wretched Anne,
      thy wife,
That never slept a quiet hour with thee,
Now fills thy sleep with **perturbations**.   worries
Tomorrow in the battle think on me,
And fall thy edgeless sword: despair and die.

                                                          [*Exit*]

Ghost of Buckingham: The first was I that help'd thee
      to the crown;
The last was I that felt thy tyranny.
O, in the battle think of Buckingham,
And die in terror of thy guiltiness.
Dream on, dream on of bloody deeds and death;
Fainting, despair: despairing, yield thy breath.

                                                          [*Exit*]

Think about it

How would you stage this scene?
Why does Shakespeare remind us of all
Richard's crimes at this point in the play?

the foe vaunts in the field – the enemy is ready for battle

A thing divised by the enemy.

Let not our babbling dreams affright our souls; conscience is but a word that cowards use to keep the strong in awe.

March on! Join bravely. Let us to it **pell-mell** – if not to Heaven, then hand in hand to hell!

Remember whom you are to cope withal: a scum of Bretons and base peasants. And who doth lead them but a paltry fellow. A milksop! Shall these enjoy our lands? Lie with our wives? Ravish our daughters? Fight, gentlemen of England! Fight, bold yeomen! Spur your proud horses hard, and ride in blood!

What says Lord Stanley?

He doth deny to come.

Off with his son George's head!

My lord, the enemy is past the marsh. After the battle let George Stanley die.

Advance our standards! Set upon our foes. Upon them! Victory sits on our helms.

pell-mell – quickly

55

Catesby urges Richard to escape but Richard refuses.

Rescue! My lord of Norfolk, rescue! The King enacts more wonders than a man. His horse is slain, and all on foot he fights, seeking for Richmond. Rescue, fair lord, or else the day is lost!

A horse! A horse! My kingdom for a horse!

Withdraw, my lord; I'll help you to a horse.

Slave! I have set my life upon a cast, and I will stand **the hazard of the die**.

I think there be six Richmonds in the field: five have I slain today instead of him.

A horse! A horse! My kingdom for a horse!

the hazard of the die – a throw of the dice

56

royalty – crown

57

Norfolk, Lord Ferrers, Brakenbury and Brandon.

Inter their bodies as become their births.

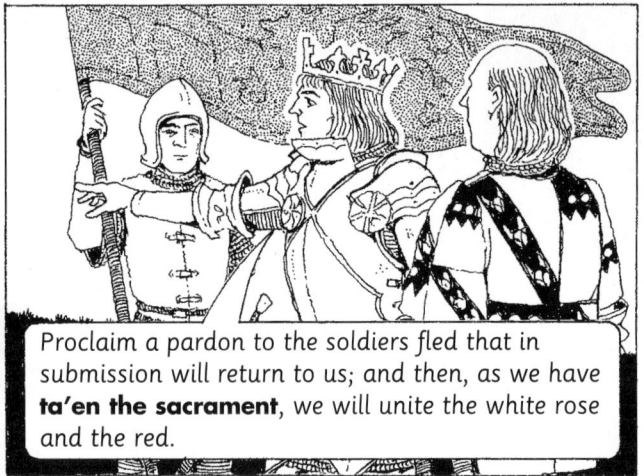

Proclaim a pardon to the soldiers fled that in submission will return to us; and then, as we have **ta'en the sacrament**, we will unite the white rose and the red.

O, now let Richmond and Elizabeth, the true succeeders of each royal House, by God's fair ordinance join together...

...and let their heirs, God, if Thy will be so, enrich the time to come with smooth-fac'd peace, with smiling plenty, and fair prosperous days.

Now civil wounds are stopp'd; peace lives again. That she may long live here, God say Amen.

THE END.

ta'en the sacrament – solemnly promised